Thinking Critically: Sexual Harassment

Other titles in the *Thinking Critically* series include:

Thinking Critically: Sexual Harassment

Stephen Currie

ReferencePoint Press®

San Diego, CA

© 2019 ReferencePoint Press, Inc.
Printed in the United States

For more information, contact:
ReferencePoint Press, Inc.
PO Box 27779
San Diego, CA 92198
www.ReferencePointPress.com

LIBRARY OF CONGRESS CATALOGING-IN-PUBLICATION DATA

Names: Currie, Stephen, 1960– author.
Title: Thinking Critically: Sexual Harassment/by Stephen Currie.
Description: San Diego, CA: ReferencePoint Press, [2018] | Series: Thinking Critically | Audience:
    Grade 9 to 12. | Includes bibliographical references and index.
Identifiers: LCCN 2018022785 (print) | LCCN 2018026188 (ebook) | ISBN 9781682824443 (eBook)
    | ISBN 9781682824436 (hardback)
Subjects: LCSH: Sexual harassment—Juvenile literature.
Classification: LCC HQ1237 (ebook) | LCC HQ1237 .C87 2018 (print) | DDC 305.42—dc23
LC record available at https://lccn.loc.gov/2018022785

Contents

Foreword

"Literacy is the most basic currency of the knowledge economy we're living in today." Barack Obama (at the time a senator from Illinois) spoke these words during a 2005 speech before the American Library Association. One question raised by this statement is: What does it mean to be a literate person in the twenty-first century?

E.D. Hirsch Jr., author of *Cultural Literacy: What Every American Needs to Know*, answers the question this way: "To be culturally literate is to possess the basic information needed to thrive in the modern world. The breadth of the information is great, extending over the major domains of human activity from sports to science."

But literacy in the twenty-first century goes beyond the accumulation of knowledge gained through study and experience and expanded over time. Now more than ever literacy requires the ability to sift through and evaluate vast amounts of information and, as the authors of the Common Core State Standards state, to "demonstrate the cogent reasoning and use of evidence that is essential to both private deliberation and responsible citizenship in a democratic republic."

The *Thinking Critically* series challenges students to become discerning readers, to think independently, and to engage and develop their skills as critical thinkers. Through a narrative-driven, pro/con format, the series introduces students to the complex issues that dominate public discourse—topics such as gun control and violence, social networking, and medical marijuana. Each chapter revolves around a single, pointed question such as Can Stronger Gun Control Measures Prevent Mass Shootings?, or Does Social Networking Benefit Society?, or Should Medical Marijuana Be Legalized? This inquiry-based approach introduces student researchers to core issues and concerns on a given topic. Each chapter includes one part that argues the affirmative and one part that argues the negative—all written by a single author. With the single-author format the predominant arguments for and against an issue can be synthesized into clear, accessible discussions supported by details and evidence including relevant facts, direct quotes, current examples, and statistical illustrations. All volumes include focus questions to guide students as they read each pro/con discussion, a list of key facts, and an annotated list of related organizations and websites for conducting further research.

The authors of the Common Core State Standards have set out the particular qualities that a literate person in the twenty-first century must have. These include the ability to think independently, establish a base of knowledge across a wide range of subjects, engage in open-minded but discerning reading and listening, know how to use and evaluate evidence, and appreciate and understand diverse perspectives. The new *Thinking Critically* series supports these goals by providing a solid introduction to the study of pro/con issues.

Sexual Harassment in the Spotlight

For many years, Harvey Weinstein was one of the most powerful figures in Hollywood. As a movie producer, he was involved in choosing directors, arranging financing, and much more. In the fall of 2017, however, the *New York Times* printed an article detailing Weinstein's history of sexual harassment against women. More than a dozen women had come forward with complaints about the producer's behavior. Temporary hires, assistants, and well-known singers and actresses (including Ashley Judd and Rose McGowan) all alleged that Weinstein had acted in inappropriately sexual ways toward them—and had threatened their livelihoods if they refused to put up with it.

These were serious allegations. While most—though not all—of the interactions described did not break any existing laws, the stories the women told were disturbing. According to Judd, for instance, Weinstein met with her in a hotel room, supposedly to discuss business, but instead requested that she watch him shower or give him a massage. Other women reported that Weinstein exposed himself to them; made sexually charged comments; groped their breasts, buttocks, or genitals; or pushed them into having sex against their better judgment. Given Weinstein's power in Hollywood, refusing his advances was dangerous. Women who did so risked losing their jobs or damaging their careers, but those who complied with Weinstein's demands might expect higher-paid positions or a greater chance at stardom. "How do I get out of the room as fast as possible without alienating Harvey Weinstein?"[1] Judd recalls asking herself.

Further Allegations

Reaction to the *Times* article was swift and angry. Weinstein quickly issued a general apology acknowledging that he had "caused a lot of pain."[2] At the same time, however, he flatly denied several of the charges and sought to downplay the importance of most of the others. He argued that he was a product of a different time, an era when sexually charged talk aimed at women was considered acceptable, even good fun. Lisa Bloom, one of Weinstein's attorneys, conceded that Weinstein was "an old dinosaur" but also insisted that he was "learning new ways."[3] However, these explanations and promises did little to stop the criticism, especially when other women began coming forward to say that they, too, had been harassed by Weinstein. In the weeks following the article, Weinstein lost his job, was sued by several of his victims, and was threatened with criminal charges. His reputation has been severely damaged.

The behaviors Weinstein supposedly engaged in were nothing new. Women working in the entertainment field have known for years about directors, producers, and fellow actors who preyed on them and demanded sexual favors. "Stars from Shirley Temple to Judy Garland faced producers and executives who flashed them or groped them,"[4] writes journalist Todd S. Purdum. What made the Weinstein situation different was that in the past the victims kept silent, fearing they would not be believed and expecting that they would suffer if they spoke out. In the Weinstein case, in sharp contrast, the victims were willing to speak up—and the rest of the world found their stories compelling.

Since the Weinstein accusers came forward, sexual harassment charges have come to light against a wide variety of public figures: radio personality Garrison Keillor, Olympic snowboarder Shaun White, actor Kevin Spacey, comedian-turned-politician Al Franken, and many others. Using the hashtag *#MeToo*, victims of sexual harassment are talking, often for the first time, about how they were abused by coworkers and employers. A cycle has been created in which victims are emboldened to talk about their own experiences, which then encourages others to share their stories. "When you have more people speaking, that always creates a tipping point,"[5] says law professor Tracy Thomas. The result is that sexual harassment, once essentially ignored by society, is now gaining serious attention. The process began, in a sense, with the Weinstein allegations, but it will certainly not end with them.

Defining Harassment

The term *sexual harassment* is a complicated one. Some people include violent sexual assault within the heading of sexual harassment, but most consider overt violence to be separate from harassment. In this more mainstream view, sexual harassment generally means unwelcome sexual attention apart from violence. The term is especially common when referring to workplaces or schools. According to the US Equal Employment Opportunity Commission, a government agency that enforces rules about fairness in the workplace, "Unwelcome sexual advances, requests for sexual favors, and other verbal or physical conduct of a sexual nature constitute sexual harassment when this conduct explicitly or implicitly affects an individual's employment, unreasonably interferes with an individual's work performance, or creates an intimidating, hostile, or offensive work environment."[6]

Sexual harassment thus covers a variety of behaviors. The repeated telling of off-color jokes or frequent comments about a woman's looks can qualify as sexual harassment, even though there is no physical contact in either of these situations. Sexual harassment also can include requests that the victim watch the harasser masturbate or that one person give the other a massage. Groping or fondling, in which harassers touch their victim for their own sexual pleasure, is another common form of sexual harassment. And sexual harassment usually includes situations in which a harasser requests sexual contact and the victim acquiesces, either in hopes of a reward (such as being cast in a movie) or for fear of being penalized (such as being fired or demoted).

Though the majority of sexual harassment is perpetrated against women, that is not invariably the case. Several high-profile men have been charged with harassing other men. Actor Kevin Spacey is perhaps the best known of these harassers. In October 2017 he was accused of having tried to assault a fourteen-year-old boy in 1986; within a few days

A 2017 New York Times article detailing a history of sexual harassment against women by powerful movie producer Harvey Weinstein (pictured) helped launch the #MeToo movement. Sexual harassment continues to get attention as a problem in many countries.

of that accusation, other men came forward with allegations of their own, among them claims of groping, a charge that Spacey had exposed himself to an unwilling observer, and an accusation that Spacey had watched pornographic videos with a teenage boy. Spacey has denied most of the accusations and claims he does not remember others. "I am beyond horrified to hear his story," Spacey wrote about his first accuser. "If I did behave as he describes, I owe him the sincerest apology for what would have been deeply inappropriate drunken behavior."[7]

Although accusations against men account for the overwhelming majority of sexual harassment charges, women have been charged with harassment as well. In February 2018, for example, California legislative aide Daniel Fierro accused state legislator Cristina Garcia of harassing him in 2014. Fierro says Garcia began by touching his arm and his upper back. "Then she dropped her hand to my butt and squeezed,"[8] he told a reporter. When he tried to walk away, Fierro says, she reached for his crotch. Other men also accused Garcia of similar behavior toward them. Though she denied all charges, Garcia agreed to take a leave of absence from her legislative job. In a few cases, women have been accused of harassment of other women too.

No matter the gender of the victim or perpetrator, one theme present in virtually all sexual harassment cases is an imbalance of power. The harasser has more power than the victim and often has direct authority over the victim as well. The harasser relies on this authority to get away with the behavior: someone who fears losing her job if she complains about harassment may decide to keep silent. "I am a 28 year old woman trying to make a living and a career," wrote Lauren O'Connor, an employee at Weinstein's company who ended up speaking out against Weinstein's abusive behavior. "Harvey Weinstein is a 64 year old, world famous man and this is his company. The balance of power is me: 0, Harvey Weinstein: 10."[9]

A Watershed Moment

There are many important debates surrounding the #MeToo movement and the pushback against sexual harassment. Some observers worry, for instance, that sexual harassers are being punished too severely. Some question whether Americans are too quick to assume the guilt of an alleged harasser. Another debate involves whether the blame for sexual harassment rests solely with the harassers or whether blame also lies with society at large. It is also unclear what will happen in the future, with some arguing that #MeToo will succeed in making sexual harassment a thing of the past and others doubting that the movement will have a lasting impact.

These debates aside, however, there is no doubt that American society has come a very long way concerning sexual harassment. The willingness of victims to come forward with their stories is unprecedented in American history. So, too, is the willingness of the public to believe these accounts and to punish the harassers. The #MeToo movement has succeeded in ways that most Americans would have thought impossible just a few years ago. Whatever the future may hold for victims of harassment, the success of #MeToo in addressing and combatting the issue has been remarkable. Where sexual harassment is concerned, Americans are truly witnessing history in the making.

Chapter One

Who Is to Blame for Sexual Harassment?

Sexual Harassment Is Mainly a Cultural Problem

- Workplace culture features an imbalance of power, which leads to harassing behavior.
- American society demeans women and fails to take them seriously.
- Sexual harassment has been prevalent throughout recent American history.
- Friends and colleagues of harassers typically support them rather than turning them in.

The Debate at a Glance

Sexual Harassment Is Fundamentally an Individual Problem

- Americans typically hold individuals, not society, responsible for their own behavior.
- Most people in positions of power, as well as most men, do not engage in sexual harassment.
- Society has changed in significant ways over time, yet sexual harassment persists.
- Sexual harassers share many negative personality traits.

Sexual Harassment Is Mainly a Cultural Problem

"This is not an individual problem. This is a systemic problem. There are no two sides. 'Personal responsibility' doesn't factor in. . . . It's a system of oppression in action."

—Carina Chocano, a writer who focuses on cultural issues

Carina Chocano, "Why the Harvey Weinstein Allegations Could Change Our Culture," *Rolling Stone*, October 19, 2017. www.rollingstone.com.

Consider these questions as you read:

1. Which quotation (or quotations) in this essay best supports the basic argument? Explain your reasoning.
2. According to the author, what aspects of American culture and society are most directly tied to sexual harassment? How so or in what way?
3. What part of this argument do you find the most compelling? What part do you find the most flawed? Explain your reasoning.

Editor's note: The discussion that follows presents common arguments made in support of this perspective, reinforced by facts, quotes, and examples taken from various sources.

The allegations against Harvey Weinstein were groundbreaking in the fight against sexual harassment for a variety of reasons. For one, victims were widely believed, which had rarely—if ever—happened before in American history. For another, the story got considerably more coverage in the media than most earlier stories of harassment. Finally, the allegations against Weinstein encouraged victims of other men to come forward to tell their stories, eventually sparking the growth of the #MeToo movement. For these reasons, the Weinstein case can be regarded as new and unusual.

Unfortunately, though, the accusations against Weinstein were neither unusual nor new. The behaviors in which Weinstein allegedly engaged have been quite common throughout American history. Retail clerks, food-service workers, middle managers, academics—no profession has been immune to sexual harassment. For years, women in all workplaces have had to contend with suggestive comments, unwanted groping, and the expectation that they would submit to sex if they wanted to be hired, promoted, or cast in a play or a movie. "Don't forget, darling, tomorrow you're going to be a star,"[10] read a plaque above a couch in a Hollywood producer's office during the 1950s.

Sexual harassment, then, runs deep in American culture—so deep, in fact, that it is fair to blame society for the appalling prevalence of harassment in the workplace. Some of the blame lies with the power-hungry men and occasional women who delight in harassing their employees. But the culture of the American workplace is the real culprit. The way women are treated in society, the role that money and status play in American life, and the willingness of observers to look the other way all serve to keep harassment under wraps. These factors make it difficult—if not impossible—for victims to tell their stories, and they discourage those with knowledge of a violation from speaking out about what they see and hear. If not for those cultural elements, the power of harassers would be blunted, perhaps even eliminated. This is why sexual harassment is primarily a systemic problem, the result of a culture that does not wish to address the issues.

The Role of Women

Many aspects of American society encourage an atmosphere in which men may feel free to harass women. Even the basic economic structure of the United States is partly to blame. Consider, for example, that women are traditionally paid less than men, even when they are doing the same work and have similar experience and skills. Moreover, men are much more likely than women to have authority over other people in the workplace. As of 2015, only about 40 percent of managers in American businesses were women—and the gap is considerably wider for especially

Sexual Harassment Is Widespread

This information is taken from a 2018 survey commissioned by an organization called Stop Street Harassment. Among other results, the study reveals that more than half of American adults say they have experienced verbal sexual harassment, and more than half of American women say they have experienced physically aggressive harassment. That so many Americans have been subjected to sexual harassment strongly suggests that something in American culture creates conditions under which harassment can thrive.

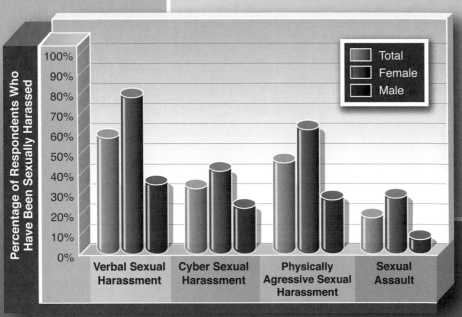

Prevalence of Sexual Harassment and Assault in the United States

Source: Stop Street Harassment, "The Facts Behind the #MeToo Movement," 2018. www.stopstreetharassment.org.

powerful positions. At the executive level, women hold only about 25 percent of manager posts, and the most powerful executives are overwhelmingly men. Only about 5 percent of the largest American companies are run by a woman.

Outside the workplace as well, women are not given the same opportunities as men. As of spring 2018, for example, the US Senate included just twenty-three women among its one hundred members, and the legislatures of virtually all states were dominated by men. With a handful of exceptions, female athletes and sports teams earn very little money and recognition compared with their male counterparts. Studies reveal that ideas are not valued as highly when they come from women as when they come from men. Females are underrepresented in history too. The Pulitzer Prize is awarded each year to a notable book about American history, but as historian Elizabeth Cobbs points out, not all history books seem to qualify. "In its first 100 years," Cobbs writes, "the Pulitzer Prize committee recognized a book focused on women's history only once. And that was a book about childbearing."[11]

The result is a culture in which women as a group lack power, authority, and a voice. These are necessary conditions for sexual harassment to thrive. Harassers are fundamentally bullies who prey on the weakest members of society. When women rarely ascend to positions of power but are instead placed in subservient roles, the situation is ripe for more powerful male supervisors to take advantage of them. When women are routinely ignored, devalued, or patronized, they will not be inclined to speak up if harassed—and they may not be believed if they do. "Most of your complaints will amount to nothing," journalist and business consultant Farva Jafri warns young women who are victims of harassment. "Women don't speak up because nobody listens."[12]

> "Most of your complaints will amount to nothing. Women don't speak up because nobody listens."[12]
>
> —Journalist and business consultant Farva Jafri

Colleagues, Friends, and Enablers

In many fields, especially those dominated by men, the problems are systemic. Jafri describes sitting in meetings where male colleagues competed to tell the dirtiest joke or make the most sexist remark. Rather than reveal her true feelings, she found it easier and safer to laugh with them, even though she found most of the banter offensive. Only after many such meetings did she find the strength to push back. One day,

Jafri writes, some of the men in a meeting she attended were making "incredibly hostile" comments about a woman she knew. "As I sat with this group of men, laughing at a young girl whose name would be tarnished at our small company," Jafri continues, "I realized I was complicit in the situation. . . . I was enabling [these] men."[13]

Indeed, harassers take advantage of this atmosphere to make their behavior appear entirely normal. Most harassment victims report that their harassers were aided by people who knew what was happening but did not feel comfortable challenging even egregious misconduct. Examples are not difficult to find. In 2017, for instance, eight women came forward alleging that talk show host Charlie Rose had harassed them by walking around naked in their presence, describing sexual fantasies involving them, and groping their buttocks, among other behaviors. One victim approached Rose's executive producer, Yvette Vega, with her concerns but was told, "That's just Charlie being Charlie."[14] Likewise, for years, Weinstein convinced the people he knew to ignore allegations of harassment against him. "Dozens of Mr. Weinstein's former and current employees, from assistants to top executives, said they knew of inappropriate conduct when they worked for him," reports the *New York Times*. "Only a handful said they ever confronted him."[15]

> "That's just Charlie being Charlie."[14]
>
> —Yvette Vega, executive producer working for accused sexual harasser Charlie Rose

The people who engage in sexual harassment are brutes, and there is no defense for what they do. Still, it is clear that a very large percentage of the blame belongs to American culture. Ours is a society in which men dominate and women are ignored; a society in which bystanders and confidantes excuse inexcusable behavior; a society in which allegations, until very recently, are more often dismissed than believed. It is worth considering how the situation would be different if the underlying culture were to change.

In 2005 Donald Trump—then a businessman and reality television performer—had a conversation with television host Billy Bush in which he used vulgar language to discuss making sexual advances toward women. No one present expressed disapproval of Trump's comments.

Michael Kimmel, who runs the Center for the Study of Men and Masculinities, wonders what might have happened had the response been different. "Imagine that Billy Bush and all those other guys said, 'Donald, that is disgusting, not to mention illegal,'" Kimmel says. "Would he still boast so much about his behavior if they said that?"[16] In the case of Trump or any specific person, there is no way to know for sure. But a reaction such as Kimmel describes would undoubtedly reduce sexual harassment in many cases.

"Imagine that Billy Bush and all those other guys said, 'Donald, that is disgusting, not to mention illegal.' Would he still boast so much about his behavior if they said that?"[16]

—Michael Kimmel, the founder of the Center for the Study of Men and Masculinities

Sexual Harassment Is Fundamentally an Individual Problem

"Just because a behavior was ignored, tolerated, or even encouraged [in the wider culture] doesn't make it remotely close to excusable."

—Eric March, a commentator for the website Upworthy

Eric March, "Let's Break Down 15 Terrible Excuses from Accused Sexual Harassers and Predators," Upworthy, November 15, 2017. www.upworthy.com.

Consider these questions as you read:

1. Based on the evidence in this argument, do you think it is possible for sexual harassment to be simultaneously an individual problem and a cultural problem? Explain.
2. According to the argument, what role does psychology play in sexual harassment?
3. What counterargument might be effective against the ideas in this essay? Why?

Editor's note: The discussion that follows presents common arguments made in support of this perspective, reinforced by facts, quotes, and examples taken from various sources.

In any given case of sexual harassment, the fault lies squarely on the shoulders of one person: the harasser. Any attempts to blame someone else, let alone an entire culture, are fundamentally misguided. Certainly, aspects of society have helped create an atmosphere in which harassers can misbehave and in which stopping them is difficult. But it was not society that carried out the harassment. Similarly, those who looked the other way while harassment was going on need to think deeply about their actions and the ethics of the choices they made. But they were not the people who engaged in the behavior. To hold anybody responsible for someone else's abusive actions is unreasonable and unfair. The fault lies with the harasser—period.

Individual Choice

On the face of it, the idea that American culture is to blame for sexual harassment has some merit. Indeed, sexism is rampant in American life, men hold most leadership positions in the workplace, and harassers have long been helped by associates who refuse to acknowledge the abusive behavior. No one would argue that these issues are insignificant. But fundamentally, the notion that some amorphous American philosophy or attitude brings about harassment is flawed. The argument clearly fails because most people, even most men, do not engage in sexual harassment. If the problem were simply one of culture and society, we would expect that the great majority of men would be sexual harassers, and that is simply not the case. While estimates vary, it seems doubtful that more than 25 percent of men harass others. Though culture may play a role, the behavior of individuals is much more significant. "Can we simply say 'boys will be boys' and explain sexual harassment as the natural extension of maleness?" asks evolutionary scientist Richard G. Bribiescas. "The answer is no. We cannot."[17]

> "Can we simply say 'boys will be boys' and explain sexual harassment as the natural extension of maleness? The answer is no. We cannot."[17]
>
> —Richard G. Bribiescas, evolutionary scientist

The culture argument falls apart in other ways as well. What exactly does it mean to say that society is to blame for harassment? "I came of age in the '60s and '70s when all the rules about behavior and workplaces were different," Harvey Weinstein explained. "That was the culture then."[18] Apparently Weinstein does not blame himself for forcing women who worked for him into uncomfortable situations or for demanding sexual favors in exchange for supporting a performer's career. Rather, Weinstein argues, society was at fault. But to accept this argument is to completely ignore the reality of individual choice. No matter how prevalent sexual harassment was when Weinstein was a young executive, he did not have to follow the lead of those around him. He could have done what was right. He made a different decision, however, and that is his responsibility alone.

In fact, Weinstein's argument is both appalling and self-serving. Not only does the argument falsely suggest that all men born at the same time as Weinstein became sexual harassers, but it also ignores the fact that the world has changed. While women still have a long way to go to be fully equal in society, they are far better off today than they were a half century ago, and behaviors and attitudes that once might have been broadly acceptable now seem to be relics from a less enlightened time. Weinstein's assertion that the 1960s and 1970s were a different era might carry some weight if he had stopped misbehaving as society's expectations changed. Of course, that is not the case: Weinstein seems to have been just as willing to harass women in 2017 as he was in 1967. The blame, then, does not lie with some vague culture in which Weinstein began his career. As political commentator Sally Kohn writes, "Make no mistake about it, Harvey Weinstein is at fault for his behaviors and the climate he created in his companies."[19]

> "Make no mistake about it, Harvey Weinstein is at fault for his behaviors and the climate he created in his companies."[19]
>
> —Sally Kohn, political commentator

The Psychology of Harassment

The psychology of men who sexually harass others also strongly suggests that they, not society, are responsible for their behavior. While no two harassers are exactly alike, the majority of those who harass others share several characteristics. Emotionally speaking, the typical harasser is not normal. Research indicates, for example, that the typical male perpetrator of sexual harassment holds unusually hostile attitudes toward women. Harassers do not typically value women's contributions in the workplace or elsewhere. They strongly agree with sweeping generalizations like "[Wearing] a short skirt means a woman is asking for [sex],"[20] and seem to delight in causing women discomfort. Men in supervisory positions who show this kind of anger and resentment are much more likely to become harassers than men whose attitudes toward women are respectful.

Sexual harassers share other traits as well. As a *Psychology Today* article notes, "Harassment indicates a willingness to exploit and manipulate as a way to maintain and gain power."[21] That is a classic definition of a bully, and indeed many bullies engage in sexual harassment as well as harassment of other kinds. Moral disengagement is another common characteristic of harassers: They find it easy to convince themselves that they are exempt from ethical behavior. Similarly, many sexual harassers are narcissists, a psychological term used to describe people who have an unreasonably high opinion of themselves. Narcissists typically lack empathy and have a powerful desire to be admired by others. These traits lead them to believe that they are entitled to get what they want, regardless of the cost to anyone else. It should be no surprise that narcissism is closely linked to harassing behavior.

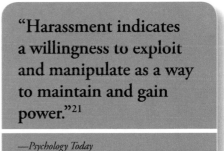

"**Harassment indicates a willingness to exploit and manipulate as a way to maintain and gain power.**"[21]

—*Psychology Today*

If societal forces were fundamentally responsible for sexual harassment, perpetrators would represent a wide variety of personality types. But they do not. Instead, harassers share a few sharply negative character traits, most obviously hostility toward women, a tendency to bully others, moral disengagement, and narcissism. These links strongly suggest that the responsibility for harassment lies with the individual, not a culture. Whereas psychologically healthy people seem able to avoid harassing others, those whose emotional lives are unhealthy are much more likely to engage in harassment. In light of this information, it seems implausible to conclude that society is at fault for sexual harassment.

Blame and Responsibility

Blaming society for sexual harassment is questionable for another reason as well. In other areas, Americans typically fix blame for bad behavior

Character Traits of Harassers

Many perpetrators of sexual harassment share certain character traits that are not found among all—or even most—members of society. Taken together, these traits strongly correlate with harassment. Since these traits are not associated with society at large, it seems evident that sexual harassment is an individual problem specific to people who share this mix of characteristics.

Trait	Description
Narcissism	The person has an excessively positive view of himself or herself coupled with a lack of empathy.
Psychopathy	The person is impulsive and enjoys exploiting others for his or her gain.
Moral disengagement	The person justifies immoral behavior, often by dehumanizing victims and blaming others for his or her actions.
Hostility toward women	The person neither likes nor respects women and sees women as objects to be manipulated.
Employment in male-dominated fields	The person holds a job in a field such as engineering, the military, or high technology.

Source: Ellen Hendriksen, "Four Psychological Traits of Sexual Harassers," *How to Be Yourself* (blog), *Psychology Today*, November 9, 2017. www.psychologytoday.com.

squarely on the perpetrator's shoulders. Drunk drivers, for example, are held accountable for the crashes they cause. Americans may decry a culture of drinking, widespread in many communities, which encourages excessive consumption of alcohol. They may question the motives of friends who did not keep the drunk person from driving once the degree of his or her impairment became clear. They might advocate for a better system of public transportation, which could lessen the need for people to use their cars even after drinking. The legal system might even bring charges against a bartender who continued to serve a customer who was obviously drunk and later caused a terrible accident. But nearly all observers would agree that the fundamental responsibility for a drunk driving accident belongs to the driver.

The sale of illegal drugs, such as opioids or cocaine, is another example. People who are caught selling banned substances are usually tried for their crimes. If found guilty, they can expect to serve time in prison. When they appear before judges and juries, drug dealers are free to argue that someone else is at fault. They can assert, if they like, that society is to blame for their decision to sell drugs. They can argue that the true culprits are the addicts who buy the drugs, or they can blame the difficulties and disappointments of life, which make many people turn to drugs to begin with. They can even blame the people who produce the drugs.

But those arrested for selling illegal substances cannot expect to sway a judge or jury with these claims. People deciding the case will see these arguments as self-centered and flawed. Indeed, they will almost invariably blame the person on trial rather than blame society, addicts, or those who make drugs. Why would sexual harassment be a societal responsibility when drug dealing and drunk driving are not? The obvious answer is that despite what some people say, sexual harassment is no more attributable to American culture than is any other crime or misbehavior. Harassers are not entitled to blame society, their friends, or anyone else. They, and they alone, are responsible for their actions.

Chapter Two

How Harshly Should Harassers Be Punished?

Sexual Harassers Must Not Be Punished Excessively

- People guilty of low-level harassment should not be punished as if they had committed major crimes.
- Destroying people's reputations and finances is a vindictive response to harassment, not a measured, thoughtful one.
- Punishments should not deprive the world of hardworking representatives or creative works.

The Debate at a Glance

Punishments for Sexual Harassers Are Not Excessive

- Many harassers are given penalties that are too mild or almost nonexistent.
- Even a harsh punishment may not be in effect for more than a few months.
- All harassment is serious and should be punished accordingly; it is not the case that there are different levels of offenses.

Sexual Harassers Must Not Be Punished Excessively

"In our current climate, to be accused [of sexual harassment] is to be convicted. Due process is nowhere to be found."

—Daphne Merkin, a critic and novelist

Daphne Merkin, "Publicly, We Say #MeToo. Privately, We Have Misgivings," *New York Times*, January 6, 2018. www.nytimes.com.

Consider these questions as you read:

1. Which anecdote or piece of evidence in this essay do you think is most effective for making the author's case? Why?
2. The text describes the loss of reputation and the loss of income as two common penalties applied to sexual harassers. Which of these do you think is a more serious punishment? Why? Explain your reasoning.
3. How seriously do you think the author of this essay takes sexual harassment? What is your evidence?

Editor's note: The discussion that follows presents common arguments made in support of this perspective, reinforced by facts, quotes, and examples taken from various sources.

Many people who have been accused of sexual harassment have paid a heavy price for their behavior, including being fined, losing their jobs, and having their reputations ruined. Indeed, accusations of improper behavior have sullied the names of many men—and a few women— who were once widely respected. Consider the case of Harvey Weinstein. Once, attaching his name to a movie guaranteed that the film would be taken seriously and increased its chance of winning a major award. That is no longer true. "His name is now mud,"[22] says Sasha Stone, who writes about the film business. Actor Kevin Spacey's reputation has also been destroyed since being accused of sexual misconduct. "His stature in the industry is over," says Elizabeth Toledo, a public relations expert. "There's no legal or [public relations] strategy that's going to restore it."[23]

On one level, sexual harassment deserves to be punished, as it demeans victims, discomforts onlookers, and damages the ideal of a free and equal society. But in our laudable zeal to stamp out sexual harassment, we are imposing punishments that are unreasonably harsh. The penalties for harassment should be thoughtful responses to bad behavior, but the punishments doled out to harassers tend to be out of line with their actual offenses.

Crimes and Punishments

There are several reasons why the penalties for sexual harassment so often seem excessive, but the most important is probably the gap between action and punishment. The issue is easy to see in the cases of men whose reputations and livelihoods have been destroyed even though their behavior was more annoying than appalling. Consider what happened when several women claimed they had been harassed by editor and literary critic Leon Wieseltier. Wieseltier, they asserted, had tried to kiss them and repeatedly made suggestive comments regarding what his female employees wore. "The only problem with that dress is that it's not tight enough,"[24] he reportedly told one woman.

> "I don't think hitting on people with whom you interact professionally is a hanging offense."[25]
>
> —Cathy Young, journalist

Wieseltier's actions were unacceptable, and his victims had every right to complain about him in public. Still, Wieseltier apparently did not force his underlings to go to bed with him, touch his female employees' breasts or buttocks, or use violence to get what he wanted. Nonetheless, Wieseltier was severely punished: he was fired from his work at a magazine and at a think tank. In addition, funding for a new magazine that was to be edited by Wieseltier was abruptly withdrawn. These penalties are inappropriate for someone who was largely engaging in unwanted flirtation. "I don't think hitting on

28

Concern About Excessive Punishment

According to a Vox/Morning Consult poll taken in early 2018, American women are worried that punishments for some forms of sexual harassment may be too harsh. The survey revealed that 56 percent of women were either "very" or "somewhat" concerned that punishments for less serious forms of sexual harassment were often the same as punishments for more serious forms. This is a problem. Bad behavior needs to be punished, but the punishment must fit the crime.

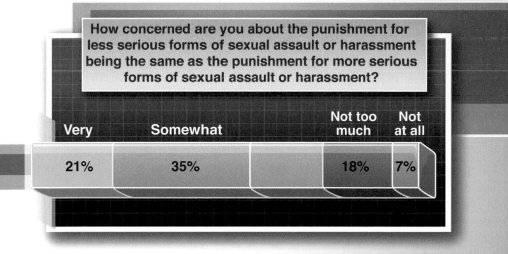

How concerned are you about the punishment for less serious forms of sexual assault or harassment being the same as the punishment for more serious forms of sexual assault or harassment?

Very	Somewhat		Not too much	Not at all
21%	35%		18%	7%

Source: Anna North, "Why Women Are Worried About #MeToo," Vox, April 5, 2018. www.vox.com.

people with whom you interact professionally is a hanging offense,"[25] writes journalist Cathy Young.

Comedian-turned-politician Al Franken is another example of a man whose punishment may have been too harsh. Franken, a former cast member and writer for the popular television show *Saturday Night Live,* became a US senator in 2008. In late 2017 a broadcaster named Leeann Tweeden charged that Franken had harassed her in 2006 while the two were on a tour performing for troops stationed abroad. In particular, she charged that while she was asleep on an airplane, Franken posed for pictures beside her. In several of the images, all taken without Tweeden's knowledge or consent, he appeared to be placing his hands on or just above her breasts.

Franken quickly apologized. Noting that he had still been working as a comedian at the time, Franken explained that the photo was not intended to offend. "It was clearly intended to be funny but wasn't," Franken admitted. "I shouldn't have done it."[26] However, other accusations followed. Several women who had posed for pictures with Franken accused him of grabbing their buttocks or breasts through their clothing. Under pressure from women's groups and his colleagues in the Senate—including some from his own party—Franken resigned his Senate seat in January 2018. Unquestionably, Franken behaved badly, and some kind of punishment seems warranted. Yet like Wieseltier, Franken paid for his transgressions as if he had committed violent sexual assault. It is hard to see how the hijinks of a professional comedian should result in the loss of a Senate seat.

A Loss to Society

Franken's story raises another issue: Who benefits from the harsh penalties applied to harassers? Even many of Franken's political opponents acknowledged that he was a hardworking, effective senator. It is difficult to see how the people of Minnesota, the state that Franken represented, are helped by the resignation of a person who took his government responsibilities seriously. "I don't approve of the behavior, but I don't necessarily think it should have been career-ending in this case,"[27] says his former constituent Melanie Hagge. Instead of forcing Franken to resign, perhaps it would have been better for the Senate to have censured him—that is, issued a statement deploring Franken's behavior without requiring him to be removed from office.

> "I don't approve of [Senator Franken's] behavior, but I don't necessarily think it should have been career-ending."[27]
>
> —Minnesota resident Melanie Hagge

Similar arguments apply to other harassers. Wieseltier's behavior was certainly inappropriate, but his writings were not. When the allegations against him surfaced, he was putting together a new magazine that would explore important issues in politics and culture. As of spring 2018, it is not clear whether this magazine will ever be published. That is a shame.

"We could use a new culture-and-politics magazine," points out journalist Rod Dreher. Dreher also notes that innocent people have been harmed in the rush to penalize Wieseltier. People who were already working on the new magazine, for example, have lost their jobs. "[The] editorial staff, which does nothing wrong," Dreher argues, "shouldn't have to pay for their boss's sins committed in other workplaces."[28]

The situation is even more acute regarding people in creative fields, such as actors and directors. Consider the case of comedian/actor Louis C.K., whose popular movies have brought pleasure to many audiences. In 2017 C.K. wrote, directed, and starred in a movie called *I Love You, Daddy*. The film was scheduled to be released in mid-November. A week before the release date, however, C.K. was accused of sexual harassment, and the film's distributors announced that they would not release *I Love You, Daddy* after all.

In addition to denying C.K. the chance to earn income from the movie, refusing to release his newest film also deprives moviegoers of the chance to see a film that they might well enjoy. The same may be said of other Hollywood figures, including Spacey. "Enjoying his work doesn't mean you tacitly endorse the alleged behaviour of Kevin Spacey the private citizen," points out psychology professor Cary Cooper in a 2017 article for the online news organization the Conversation. Yet, Cooper notes, many people are now uncomfortable admitting that they like or watch Spacey's films.

The punishments given to harassers, then, are often excessive. The penalties are out of line with the behaviors, especially considering that not all harassment is equally harmful. The penalties also deprive the public of talented writers and editors such as Wieseltier, dedicated government officials like Franken, and the works of creative people like Louis C.K. It is reasonable and necessary to punish sexual harassers for their bad behavior. But we run the risk of harming all of society, not just harassers, when we impose the kinds of punishments that are common today.

> "[The] editorial staff, which does nothing wrong, shouldn't have to pay for their boss's sins committed in other workplaces."[28]
>
> —Journalist Rod Dreher on Leon Wieseltier's startup magazine being defunded

Punishments for Sexual Harassers Are Not Excessive

"To welcome someone like [comedian Louis] C.K. or [chef Mario] Batali back into the fold not six months after these accusations broke is to intimidate other victims from speaking out, because it will make them think their stories don't matter."

—Lindsay Zoladz, a cultural commentator for the website the Ringer

Lindsay Zoladz, "The #MeToo Mudslide," Ringer, April 19, 2018. www.theringer.com.

Consider these questions as you read:

1. What reasons does the author give to explain why some punishments seem heavier than others? What other explanations might there be for this phenomenon?
2. Which pieces of supporting evidence used by the author in this essay do you find most compelling? Why?
3. What is the purpose of including information about Shaun White in this essay? How does White's case strengthen the argument?

Editor's note: The discussion that follows presents common arguments made in support of this perspective, reinforced by facts, quotes, and examples taken from various sources.

Many people argue that the penalties given to sexual harassers are excessive, and in a few specific cases, there may be some truth to this charge. The shunning of Leon Wieseltier may have gone too far; perhaps it was neither necessary nor helpful to destroy his livelihood and reputation over flirtatious behaviors that journalist Michelle Cottle calls "low-level lechery."[29] Celebrity chef Mario Batali was fired from a television cooking show after a dozen women accused him of harassment in late 2017. In addition, several stores discontinued sales of his pasta sauce and cookbooks. Some suggest that being fired was sufficient and that the refusal to sell Batali's products was needlessly vindictive, and they may be right.

But when people focus on an occasional excessive penalty, they lose sight of two larger truths about punishment and sexual harassment. First, for every harasser whose punishment seems too harsh, there is at least one other whose penalty is, if anything, too mild. Second, many people see harassment mostly as a nuisance; but even when it may appear relatively insignificant, harassment is a source of great pain for the people who experience it. To say that penalties for sexual harassment are disproportionate to the offense is to deny the serious impact harassment has on its victims.

Harassers Are More Often Unpunished than Overly Punished

The notion that punishments for sexual harassment are overly harsh is misguided, in part because many harassers are scarcely penalized at all. An excellent example is snowboarder Shaun White, a three-time Olympic gold medalist. In 2016 White—who is also a musician—was sued for sexual harassment by Lena Zawaideh, who was once a drummer in White's band. In her lawsuit, Zawaideh alleged that White had "repeatedly sexually harassed her and forced his authoritarian management style on her for over seven years."[30] Among other behaviors, she claimed that White had sent her offensive text messages and forced her to watch sexually disturbing videos. Though White initially denied most of the charges, he eventually admitted to sending inappropriate texts. He settled the lawsuit out of court in 2017.

However, White has not been dogged by the charges against him. Not only was he permitted to compete at the 2018 Olympics, but he was one of the major stars highlighted in television coverage of the games that year. Even in a post-Weinstein world, announcers made no mention of the charges as the snowboarding competition was unfolding. When White was asked about Zawaideh's allegations at a press conference following the gold medal ceremony, he dismissed the charges as "gossip"[31] and was supported by the moderator, who refused to allow further questions on

Harassers Are Seldom Punished

In October 2017 ABC News and the *Washington Post* published a survey about the prevalence of sexual harassment in the United States. One of the poll's findings was that 95 percent of women who have been sexually harassed at work say that harassers usually are not punished for their actions.

Harassers Are Usually Punished

5%

Harassers Usually Go Unpunished

95%

Source: Gary Langer, "Unwanted Sexual Advances Not Just a Hollywood, Weinstein Story, Poll Finds," ABC News, October 17, 2017. https://abcnews.go.com.

the topic. In the end, White's harassment of Zawaideh cost him no sponsorships and scarcely damaged his reputation at all. Society, writes journalist Dylan Hernandez, has chosen to "celebrate [White] as an Olympic champion and relegate his transgressions to an annotated footnote."[32] It is difficult to argue that penalties for harassment are too harsh when White's reputation and livelihood remained relatively unaffected.

White is not alone in avoiding consequences for inappropriate behavior. President Donald Trump, after all, has been accused of sexual harassment by more than a dozen women, in addition to what the *Washington Post* called his "extremely lewd conversation"[33] with television personality Billy Bush that came to light in 2016. If punishments given to harassers were typically too harsh, Trump would have suffered major personal and political consequences for the allegations against him. He might have lost the endorsement of his political party, or lost the election, if voters decided they did not wish to put a sexual harasser in the White House. But although a few party members denounced him, Trump remained on the ballot, was elected president later that year, and, as of spring 2018, had faced no significant consequences for his behavior. As the cases of White and Trump demonstrate, overly harsh punishments are not the norm.

Timing and Punishment Length

Timing plays a role in punishment too. The most draconian penalties against harassers have been those given to men who were accused during the fall of 2017, a list that includes Kevin Spacey, Louis C.K., Al Franken, Harvey Weinstein, and several others. At that point the issue of sexual harassment was still quite new, and the allegations had the power to appall those who were hearing about the problem for the first time. In contrast, newer allegations have not typically resulted in the same level of attention. "Even in the era of #MeToo, a growing number of sexual harassment cases are fading from view,"[34] says journalist Jeff A. Green. Perhaps because of this dwindling focus, more recent cases have not typically resulted in the same level of punishment.

White, again, is an excellent example. Though he won his most recent Olympic medal just four months after the Weinstein allegations, few people seemed to care that he had once been charged with harassment. Evidently, advertisers, sports officials, and the general public had stopped paying close attention to the issue of harassment. As a result, White managed to avoid the punishments that were attached to other harassers whose behaviors had been called out several months earlier. If White is any indication, the problem going forward will not be that punishments are too harsh but rather that punishments are virtually nonexistent.

> "Even in the era of #MeToo, a growing number of sexual harassment cases are fading from view."[34]
>
> —Jeff A. Green, journalist

As attention shifts away from the issue of sexual harassment, it is also possible that current penalties will be shortened or relaxed. During the months following the allegations against Louis C.K., for example, C.K.

stopped giving public performances, and his newly completed movie was pulled from distribution. At the time it seemed that C.K.'s career might be over—a punishment that struck many as unnecessarily severe. It is no longer clear, however, that C.K. will remain out of the limelight for long. In the spring of 2018 entertainment reporters were speculating that C.K. would start performing in clubs by the end of the year and that his movie might soon be released as well. "I don't think people want this to be a life sentence,"[35] said comedy club owner Noam Dworman. If true, C.K.'s punishment could amount to a one-year suspension, which does not seem unduly harsh.

Levels of Harassment

Finally, the argument that penalties are too harsh typically rests on a pair of dangerous assumptions: first, that there are easily identifiable levels of harassment; and second, that all victims of harassment should respond the same way. Claims that punishments are too harsh often assume that a woman who is told an off-color joke, for example, has less reason to be offended than a woman whose boss comments on the size of her bust, and that both are better off than a woman whose supervisor gropes her.

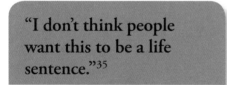

"I don't think people want this to be a life sentence."[35]

—Comedy club owner Noam Dworman on the shunning of comedian Louis C.K.

Similarly, these arguments assume that a woman who hears a suggestive comment should be able to shrug it off and move on without much difficulty.

But life is rarely so unambiguous. Different people can and do have wildly varying reactions to all kinds of experiences, one of which is sexual harassment. It is rude and paternalistic for people who have not experienced harassment to tell victims what they should be feeling. That is especially true when the underlying message is that their feelings are overblown. "Stop telling us that verbal sexual harassment isn't a big deal," writes college student Maggie Schmitt. "I'm not saying that . . . rape and verbal sexual harassment are the same kind of abuse, but both need to be treated seriously."[36]

A punishment that seems excessively harsh for the level of offense, in this view, may in fact be entirely appropriate. Responding to the notion that there are different degrees of harassment, #MeToo supporter Alyssa Milano draws an analogy with cancer. "There are different stages of cancer," she writes. "Some are more treatable than others. But it's still cancer."[37] Any apparent disconnect between penalty and offense should be resolved not by lessening the punishment but by truly recognizing the seriousness of the offense. Society owes it to the victims of harassment to do just that.

> "There are different stages of cancer. Some are more treatable than others. But it's still cancer."[37]
>
> —Alyssa Milano, an actress and #MeToo supporter, giving an analogy to sexual harassment

Chapter Three

Are We Too Quick to Assume That Accused Harassers Are Guilty?

Those Accused of Harassment Are Often Unfairly Judged

- People accused of sexual harassment should be presumed innocent until proven guilty—though they often are not.
- The penalties for harassment are serious, and a false accusation, if widely believed, can be extremely damaging.
- Although supposed victims usually tell the truth, it is unwise to assume that they always do.
- Today's culture of rapid-fire trial by social media amounts to vigilante justice when it comes to accusations of sexual harassment.

The Debate at a Glance

Those Accused of Harassment Are Fairly Judged

- Accusations of sexual assault are seldom false, and the same is likely true of sexual harassment allegations.
- It is rare that an innocent person is wrongly punished for sexual misbehavior.
- Assuming that victims are telling the truth is the best way to ensure justice.
- The price of coming forward as a victim is personally and professionally high; thus, it is not done lightly.

Those Accused of Harassment Are Often Unfairly Judged

"Lives are being put in jeopardy without a hearing, due process or evidence. . . . [To] tear each other down and destroy careers based on mere allegations is not productive at all."

—Actor and producer Jeremy Piven after being accused of sexual harassment

Quoted in Brendan O'Neill, "Whatever Happened to the Presumption of Innocence?," *Los Angeles Times*, November 16, 2017. www.latimes.com.

Consider these questions as you read:

1. Do you think there are situations in which a person should be presumed guilty? When? Do charges of sexual harassment fit this category?
2. To what extent do you agree that "society does not always tread as carefully as it should" when assuming alleged harassers are guilty? Explain.
3. Which quotation in the essay do you think most effectively supports the argument? Why?

Editor's note: The discussion that follows presents common arguments made in support of this perspective, reinforced by facts, quotes, and examples taken from various sources.

Most accusations of sexual harassment are made about an encounter that took place in a private setting—an office, a hotel room, an apartment— where only two people were present. Unless the encounter was recorded, only those two people know exactly what took place; there is no independent corroboration of what either party said or did. If those involved have wildly different stories about what happened—if one person claims to have been a victim of sexual harassment, and the other claims to have done nothing wrong—then it is incumbent upon courts, employers, and the general public to determine the truth. This is no easy task.

Although difficult, it is essential to get as close to this truth as possible—and to do so in a fair and evenhanded way. Unfortunately, *fair* and *evenhanded* do not accurately describe the process used today. Instead, many people automatically assume that all charges of harassment are true. Consider the extensive media coverage of the sexual harassment scandals in the fall of 2017. There is general agreement among Americans that most, if not all, of the women who accused men like chef Mario Batali and Hollywood mogul Harvey Weinstein were telling the truth, and there is likewise general agreement that sexual harassment is a serious problem. Still, Americans must not suspend their critical-thinking abilities when they learn about a new accusation because the allegation may not be true. Society is too quick to find accused harassers guilty as charged—and this is a serious problem.

Proof and Doubt

It should be noted that the facts of many sexual harassment cases are not in doubt. In some cases, photographic evidence exists. For example, the pictures of Al Franken in a suggestive pose above a sleeping woman make it clear that he was indeed guilty of the accusation. In other cases, harassers have admitted wrongdoing. After being accused of harassment and other forms of sexual misconduct in late 2017, for example, filmmaker Morgan Spurlock conceded that the charges were accurate. "I would call my female assistant 'hot pants' or 'sex pants' when I was yelling to her from the other side of the office," he explained. "I thought [it] was funny at the time, but then realized I had completely demeaned and belittled her to a place of non-existence."[38]

> "I am dismayed that the *New Yorker* has decided to characterize a respectful relationship with a woman I was dating as somehow inappropriate."[39]
>
> —Ryan Lizza, a journalist accused of sexual harassment

However, more difficult are cases in which the accused harasser does not admit wrongdoing and when there is no clear evidence to indicate guilt. These cases do exist. Journalist Ryan Lizza, for example, was fired

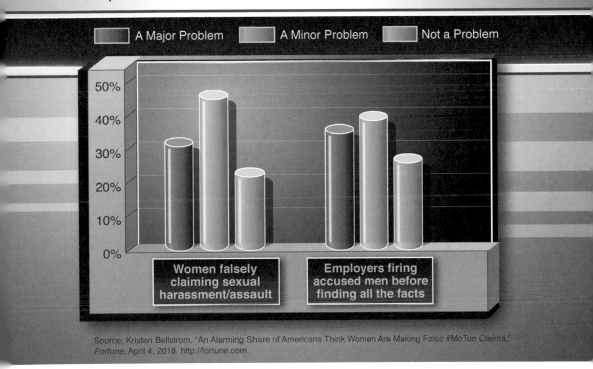

Poll Respondents Say False Accusations Are an Issue

It is difficult to find reliable information about the number of sexual harassment charges that turn out to be false. A 2018 Pew Research poll, however, revealed that a majority of Americans believe that false accusations are a problem. In addition, most poll respondents worried that men were sometimes fired by their employers before all the facts of a particular case became known.

A Major Problem   A Minor Problem   Not a Problem

50%
40%
30%
20%
10%
0%

Women falsely claiming sexual harassment/assault

Employers firing accused men before finding all the facts

Source: Kristen Bellstrom. "An Alarming Share of Americans Think Women Are Making False #MeToo Claims." *Fortune*, April 4, 2018. http://fortune.com.

from the *New Yorker* magazine after being accused of harassment by one of his female colleagues. Lizza forcefully denies any harassment, explaining that his behavior was perfectly innocent. "I am dismayed," he wrote in a statement following his firing, "that the *New Yorker* has decided to characterize a respectful relationship with a woman I was dating as somehow inappropriate."[39] In situations like these, where there is little or no outside evidence available, it is important to tread very carefully to determine the guilt or innocence of a supposed harasser. Unfortunately, society does not always tread as carefully as it should.

The Presumption of Innocence

Assuming that charges of sexual harassment are true goes against an important principle of American law: people charged with criminal behavior are innocent until they are proven guilty. That maxim protects defendants from the whims of an unfair court system. "The prosecution must prove, beyond a reasonable doubt, each essential element of the crime charged,"[40] reads an explanation of the principle in a legal dictionary. These protections mean that a defendant cannot be found guilty just because his or her guilt seems *likely*; rather, there must be no plausible alternative explanation. That principle—sometimes called the presumption of innocence—dates back hundreds of years and has long been an important part of American legal thinking and the justice system.

> "The prosecution must prove, beyond a reasonable doubt, each essential element of the crime charged."[40]
>
> —The Legal Information Institute

Not every sexual harassment case is a legal case, and very few are brought to criminal court. In the so-called court of public opinion, however, it remains sensible to presume innocence—though in an era when news travels quickly and the truth is not always valued or clear, this is rarely done. People are in such a hurry to declare an alleged harasser guilty that they ignore any possibility that he or she might be innocent. But even those whose guilt seems obvious should not be assumed guilty. When the accusations against Weinstein began to pile up, only a few voices spoke up in favor of caution and the presumption of innocence. "I'm a believer that you wait until this thing gets to trial," movie director Oliver Stone said about Weinstein as the accusations against the producer reached a peak. "I believe a man shouldn't be condemned by a vigilante system."[41]

Stone is correct: In our rush to support the victims of harassment, we sometimes trample on the rights and the needs of the accused. Not only is this situation unfair, but the penalties applied to those charged with harassment can ruin a reputation built over the course of a lifetime. In 2018 two former employees of NBC News alleged that longtime news anchor Tom Brokaw had harassed them during the 1990s. Brokaw vehemently denied the charges and was appalled that many in the media accepted them uncritically. "I was ambushed and then perp walked [treated as a criminal] across the pages of the *Washington Post* and *Variety*," Brokaw complained in a letter to some of his colleagues. "[I was] stripped of any honor and achievement I had earned in more than a half century of journalism and citizenship."[42]

No Rush to Judgment

Brokaw's situation is especially instructive because many believe he may be innocent. Some of Brokaw's female colleagues at NBC were quick to defend him when they learned of the accusations against him, for example. More than sixty of these women, including MSNBC political commentators Andrea Mitchell and Rachel Maddow—both strong supporters of the #MeToo movement—signed a letter supporting Brokaw and explaining that they had difficulty believing the charges. Brokaw, they wrote, "has treated each of us with fairness and respect."[43] Of course, behaving properly to a group of women during the 2000s does not mean Brokaw could not have behaved very differently to other women decades

earlier, and charges against Brokaw may turn out to be completely justified. But they may also prove false, and the fact that many women think this may be the case should give any reasonable person pause before assuming that Brokaw's accusers must be telling the truth.

This is not to say that accusers are lying; in fact, it is likely that many are

> "I'm a believer that you wait until this thing gets to trial. I believe a man shouldn't be condemned by a vigilante system."[41]
>
> —Oliver Stone, movie director

not. No one can be sure how many, but studies of sexual assault conclude that the majority of women who say they have been raped are telling the truth. This makes it likely that nearly all of those who say they have been victims of sexual harassment are telling the truth—but *nearly all* is not *all*. Americans must remember that occasional accusers may be delusional, seeking attention, or motivated by a desire to get someone in trouble. Given the stakes for those falsely accused, it is essential to avoid making quick judgments about whether a harassment claim is legitimate.

Those Accused of Harassment Are Fairly Judged

"I'm actually not at all concerned about innocent men losing their jobs over false sexual assault/ harassment allegations. If some innocent men's reputations have to take a hit in the process of undoing the patriarchy, that is a price I am absolutely willing to pay."

—Emily Lindin, a columnist for *Teen Vogue*

Quoted in Bari Weiss, "The Limits of 'Believe All Women,'" *New York Times*, November 28, 2017. www.nytimes.com.

Consider these questions as you read:

1. Which of the author's arguments do you find most persuasive? The least? Explain.
2. What do you find to be the greatest flaw in the author's reasoning as stated? Why?
3. The introductory paragraphs of this essay describe the experience of sexual harassment. What is the purpose of including these paragraphs?

Editor's note: The discussion that follows presents common arguments made in support of this perspective, reinforced by facts, quotes, and examples taken from various sources.

Any discussion of sexual harassment must begin with a clear understanding of how awful it is to be harassed. No office worker should ever have to put up with being in a meeting where coworkers are making sexually charged comments. No factory worker should need to deal with repeated requests for sex from a supervisor. No hotel housekeeper should have to worry that a customer will try to corner her and run his hand across her breasts or buttocks. Whatever form it takes, sexual harassment is demeaning, uncomfortable, and deeply harmful to a victim's self-image and willingness to trust others.

Until recently, moreover, the potential consequences of speaking up about sexual harassment only made things worse. Victims often did not fight back—and many continue to avoid fighting back—for fear of losing their jobs. Many, after all, rely on the goodwill of their supervisors for continued employment. Especially for poorer victims and those whose families rely on their incomes, it sometimes may seem easier to endure personal comments, dirty jokes, or an occasional demand for a kiss than to face the prospect of suddenly being unemployed.

Moreover, when victims have fought back, they have traditionally not been believed. Consider the case of Crystal Washington, who served as the hospitality coordinator at a fancy hotel and was delighted at first to have gotten her job. Her experience soured quickly, though, when a coworker began making sexually charged comments to Washington and touching her inappropriately. When

> "It's a dream to be an employee there. And then you find out what it really is, and it's a nightmare."[44]
>
> —Crystal Washington, a hotel employee whose claims of sexual harassment were ignored by her supervisors

she told him to stop, he did not. Unlike many other women, Washington brought her complaints to management, noting that one of these encounters had actually been caught on a security camera. But in her opinion, management did nothing to stop the harassing behavior. "It's a dream to be an employee there," Washington says of the hotel. "And then you find out what it really is, and it's a nightmare."[44]

Indeed, the word *nightmare* sums up what sexual harassment is all about. Sexual harassment is an all-too-common experience that leaves its victims—mainly women—feeling dirty, used, and ignored. Sexual harassers deny their behavior, and if caught, they typically try to blame their victims. The victim, they say, should not have dressed the way she did, or she should have complained about the fondling on the spot instead of waiting for weeks, months, or years. Often the harassers are supported by colleagues, friends, and others who agree that the victim is at fault. This attitude is not a thing of the past; it is easy to find examples of twenty-first-century men and even women who blame victims for the harassment they receive. "We must sometimes take blame, women," says actress Angela Lansbury. "I really do think that."[45] Fashion designer Donna Karan agrees. "You look at everything all over the world today, you know," she says, "and how women are dressing and what they're asking by just presenting themselves the way they do. What are they asking for? Trouble."[46] Sexual harassment, then, is itself a miserable experience in every conceivable way—and the response by harassers, observers, and the general public does nothing to help heal its victims.

False Accusations

Given this background, it is difficult to have much sympathy for people who say that society is too quick to assume the guilt of alleged harassers. Lodging a complaint against a harasser takes courage and perseverance, and the consequences for doing so can be life altering—and not in a positive way. Thus, reporting sexual harassment is not an action that victims undertake lightly. This alone strongly suggests that allegations of harassment are much more likely to be real than to be fictional. Extremely few people would willingly risk unemployment, blame, and attacks on their character to make up a story about how they were harassed.

Certainly, it is possible that some small number of harassment allegations are untrue. But the available evidence suggests that false accusations, if they exist at all, are rare indeed. Celebrities have often initially denied harassment charges, only to admit later on that they are valid. Snowboarder Shaun White, for instance, insisted at first that he had never sexually harassed his bandmate, but he conceded months later that he had in fact sent her sexually charged text messages.

> "You look at everything all over the world today, you know, and how women are dressing and what they're asking by just presenting themselves the way they do. What are they asking for? Trouble."[46]
>
> —Fashion designer Donna Karan

46

False Claims of Sexual Assault Are Uncommon

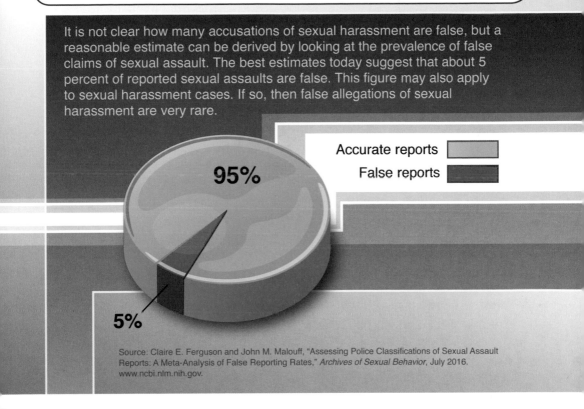

It is not clear how many accusations of sexual harassment are false, but a reasonable estimate can be derived by looking at the prevalence of false claims of sexual assault. The best estimates today suggest that about 5 percent of reported sexual assaults are false. This figure may also apply to sexual harassment cases. If so, then false allegations of sexual harassment are very rare.

Accurate reports

False reports

95%

5%

Source: Claire E. Ferguson and John M. Malouff, "Assessing Police Classifications of Sexual Assault Reports: A Meta-Analysis of False Reporting Rates," *Archives of Sexual Behavior*, July 2016. www.ncbi.nlm.nih.gov.

In other cases, witnesses have come forward to verify the victims' stories. Several of Weinstein's accusers, for instance, told friends what Weinstein did to them at the time the harassment occurred. Thus, to assume that these victims are lying about Weinstein's behavior requires the assumption that these friends are lying as well.

Other evidence also makes it unlikely that more than a small handful of harassment allegations are false. In some situations, the sheer number of victims with similar accounts strongly suggests that the charges are real. Movie director James Toback, for example, was accused of harassment by multiple women in October 2017. Toback has claimed that he never harassed anyone. Yet during that month alone, thirty-eight women came forward with stories—all very much alike—describing how Toback promised to help them break into the film business, only to use them sexually and then disappear. In particular, Toback seems to have enjoyed asking his victims about their masturbation habits and their pubic hair. "It was disgusting and embarrassing,"[47] said one victim, and others agree. Again, it is far more likely that Toback is guilty as charged than it is that thirty-eight women, mostly unacquainted with each other, got together to make up allegations against him.

Punishment and Justice

There are no statistics showing how many claims of sexual harassment turn out to be false, but in the United States at least, charges of the more serious offense of sexual assault are very seldom made up. According to some studies, only 2 percent of all accusations of rape prove to be unfounded. Moreover, false rape charges rarely result in an innocent man being sent to prison. According to one study, since 1989 just fifty-two men had been convicted of rape but were later found to have been falsely accused. That is an average of less than two a year. There is no good reason to suspect that the rate of false accusations is significantly different where sexual harassment is concerned.

> "It was disgusting and embarrassing."[47]
>
> —A woman who alleges that director James Toback sexually harassed her

In truth, the penalties are rarely devastating for people believed to be harassers. Going to prison for harassment is almost unheard-of, and other punishments are reversible. If evidence comes to light that someone was innocent after all, an accuser can be sued for false allegations, a business can be built back up again, a person could be rehired, and a reputation can be restored. Is it possible that an innocent person will be seriously harmed by a false allegation of sexual harassment? Yes—but it is very unlikely.

In any case, although no one ever wants to see a person harmed by a false accusation, Americans must keep in mind the context of this discussion. For years, victims of sexual harassment have been abused and silenced, blamed and mocked. They have been repeatedly denied justice for the harm done to them. Their harassers, again and again, have avoided any consequences for their behavior. Yes, it would be a shame and an injustice if even one innocent person were penalized for a false sexual harassment allegation. But injustice has been going on for years, and until recently no one seemed to care. Now is the time to support and encourage victims who come forward. If Americans truly want justice, they should start from the assumption that victims are telling the truth, uncomfortable as that may be, rather than bending over backward to give the accused the benefit of the doubt.

Chapter Four

Will Sexual Harassment Remain a Significant Problem in the Future?

Sexual Harassment Will Remain a Significant Problem in the Future

- History and human nature suggest that the powerful will always harass the powerless.
- The #MeToo movement lacks clear leaders and coherent goals.
- Most of the focus on harassment has been on celebrities, and the movement has had little or no effect on lower-profile workers.

The Debate at a Glance

Sexual Harassment Will Be Sharply Reduced in the Future

- The penalties imposed on harassers today will deter future harassers.
- Victims of harassment are increasingly willing to speak up and are frequently believed, making it harder for harassers to get away with their behavior.
- The #MeToo movement does not need designated leaders to be successful, and it has clear goals that have already been achieved.

Sexual Harassment Will Remain a Significant Problem in the Future

"#MeToo is useful, it puts the problem in the public domain. But a hashtag doesn't solve the problem."

—British historian and broadcaster Mary Beard

Quoted in Michael Hodges, "Civilisations Presenter Mary Beard: 'I'm Really Glad I Didn't Do TV Until I was 50,'" *Radio Times*, April 13, 2018. www.radiotimes.com.

Consider these questions as you read:

1. Why does the author draw connections between #MeToo and other social movements in this essay? What point(s) is he trying to make in doing so?
2. This essay makes several references to victims in low-profile jobs. What point is the author making by referring to such victims?
3. Would you characterize the essay's main argument as realistic or as overly cynical? Why?

Editor's note: The discussion that follows presents common arguments made in support of this perspective, reinforced by facts, quotes, and examples taken from various sources.

For some observers, the allegations of sexual harassment that were leveled in late 2017 and 2018 against a host of celebrities represented a major turning point in history. Unfortunately, that conclusion is difficult to support. Much more likely, the #MeToo movement will prove to be a blip, and the rapid increase in attention paid to sexual harassment will not last. It would be wonderful if that were not the case—if sexual harassment truly were on its way out—but the reality is otherwise.

The notion that harassment will wither and die under the watchful gaze of #MeToo is naïve. #MeToo has value, and it may make some small, lasting changes in how Americans think about sexual harassment.

However, it cannot make many inroads against an entrenched system in which powerful people routinely take advantage of their employees. Sexual harassment will not disappear merely because people wish it to.

Harassment and Human Nature

Sexual harassment is unlikely to go away in large part because human nature does not change much. Harassment takes place when people who hold power over others choose to use their authority in unhealthy and demeaning ways. Unfortunately, power has a negative effect on most people. The wealthy and powerful often believe that they are entitled to whatever they want and will go to great lengths to obtain it. History is full of examples. Some are especially appalling: in his twelve years as leader of Germany, Adolf Hitler caused the deaths of millions by starting a world war and attempting to exterminate Jews, homosexuals, the disabled, and other groups he disliked. But others have caused turbulence on a much smaller scale, bending rules and laws to suit their interests, making employees' lives miserable, and being willing to utterly destroy an opponent's reputation for any gain at all. As the British historian Lord Acton accurately observed more than a century ago, "All power tends to corrupt."[48]

> "All power tends to corrupt."[48]
>
> —British historian Lord Acton

Acton's observation is increasingly borne out by science. Modern research points to the corrosive effects of power, even the relatively limited power that appears in business or social settings. "Power blinds you to others' perspectives,"[49] reports an article in the online news outlet *Quartz* about the relationship between authority, harassment, and the brain. As one researcher quoted in the article notes, "Power leads people to objectify other people [and] see them in instrumental terms."[50] Thus, people in power may view an employee not so much as a person but rather as someone who can be manipulated and used. Given these circumstances, it is easy for a person in authority to begin sexually harassing people under his or her supervision.

Not all people in positions of authority mistreat those around them, of course, but the sad fact is that many do. Foreseeing a quick end to sexual harassment means believing that human nature will change more or less overnight. That seems implausible. People react to power in certain ways, and raising consciousness about sexual harassment seems unlikely to do much to stop those reactions. Is it conceivable that a concerted effort to publicize harassment and shame the perpetrators will make potential harassers think twice about their behavior? Of course. But thousands of years of history, along with what we know about brain science, suggests otherwise.

Leadership and Goals

Another reason for doubting the ultimate success of the #MeToo movement has to do with leadership. The movement "doesn't have a leader," notes an article in *Time* magazine, "or a single, unifying tenet."[51] Neither victims nor advocates have emerged to give the antiharassment forces a recognizable face. A handful of women have been deeply involved in the movement, including activist and youth worker Tarana Burke, who began using the phrase *Me Too* as part of her work with sexual assault victims in Alabama in 2006; and Alyssa Milano, an actress who popularized the term on social media in 2017. But few Americans associate the names and faces of these women specifically with #MeToo or the more general attack on sexual harassment.

That is an issue because history shows that an identifiable figurehead is of great value to a successful social movement. The civil rights movement of the 1960s, most notably, was led by many well-known people, including Martin Luther King Jr., Fannie Lou Hamer, Rosa Parks, and Malcolm X. These men and women captured newspaper headlines, strategized, and attracted sympathizers to the movement. Other examples of American movements that were successful in large part because of their leaders include the push for women's suffrage, which was led largely by famous women such as Susan B. Anthony; and the fight for the rights of migrant workers, which was headed by Mexican American labor leader Cesar Chavez.

In contrast, movements without an easily identifiable leader tend to fail. A recent example was Occupy Wall Street, which began during the

Sexual Harassment Is Underreported

According to the Equal Employment Opportunity Commission, about 70 percent of workers who are victimized by sexual harassment never report their harassers to anyone in authority at their workplaces. The current outcry against harassment may reduce this figure somewhat, but as the statistic makes clear, victims have silently put up with improper behavior for many years. It is difficult to imagine this changing dramatically in the near future.

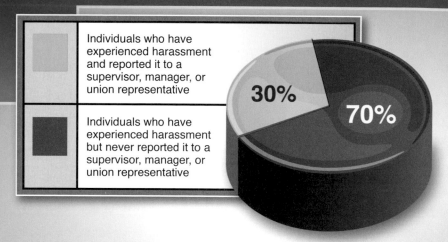

Individuals who have experienced harassment and reported it to a supervisor, manager, or union representative

Individuals who have experienced harassment but never reported it to a supervisor, manager, or union representative

30%

70%

Source: Chai R. Feldblum and Victoria A. Lipnic, "Select Task Force on the Study of Harassment in the Workplace," US Equal Employment Opportunity Commission, June 2016. www.eeoc.gov.

fall of 2011 and was designed to combat economic inequality. As journalist Andy Ostroy writes, however, Occupy Wall Street quickly "spiraled into irrelevance." Many commentators blame the movement's failure on its structure. A principal tenet of the movement was that it appointed no official leaders, preferring instead to adopt a democratic process in which everyone's voice was equal. That was an unwise strategy. "Every successful protest movement needs a leader," Ostroy points out, "a strong, passionate, articulate, visible face and voice of the movement."[52] Without leaders, #MeToo is in danger of following in Occupy Wall Street's footsteps and failing to achieve its promise.

To succeed, protest movements also need clear and unambiguous goals, and in this area #MeToo also falls short. Again, a comparison with the civil rights movement is instructive. Civil rights protesters wanted specific changes in laws, notably ensuring ballot access for African Americans and ending segregation, which was the practice of keeping blacks and whites apart in schools, theaters, and other institutions. In contrast, like Occupy Wall Street, the #MeToo movement to date has had somewhat amorphous goals. It is difficult to determine what specific legislation members of the movement want passed, for example, or which political candidates the movement might support. Until and unless the #MeToo movement develops clear leadership and specific objectives, it seems unlikely to succeed.

Celebrities and Others

To date, moreover, the national focus on sexual harassment has been very narrow. "The only women, the only men typically spoken about in the media are celebrities,"[53] points out attorney Jack Tuckner. There is no doubt that Tuckner is correct. Of the men best known for being accused of sexual harassment, virtually all are well-known for other reasons as well. Harvey Weinstein is an extremely wealthy man whose name is known throughout Hollywood. Mario Batali is a celebrity chef whose cooking products and television shows have put him squarely in the public eye. Al Franken is a former comedian and a politician, Matt Lauer is a well-known talk show host, and Mark Halperin is a journalist and best-selling author who made frequent appearances on television shows.

As a result, the media rarely if ever reports on sexual harassment involving people who do not work in high-profile fields. That is the case even though harassment in workplaces, such as restaurants, hotels, and factories, is far more common than in the entertainment industry. The sympathy and support offered to people who have been harassed by the rich and famous is entirely appropriate. But the focus has been so squarely on famous victims that no one seems especially concerned with the plight of lower-profile victims. "Having the guts to speak out if you're a working

> "The only women, the only men typically spoken about in the media are celebrities."[53]
>
> —Jack Tuckner, attorney

woman," writes David Fagin of the *Huffington Post*, "is still no easier for the average woman than it was before the hashtag [that is, the start of the #MeToo movement]."[54]

The emphasis on celebrity can help raise the profile of the #MeToo movement, and that is undoubtedly a good thing. The difficulty, as Fagin makes clear, is that such a heavy focus on high-profile cases does nothing to address sexual harassment in less sensational cases. It may be that #MeToo will succeed in limiting harassment carried out by Hollywood producers, US senators, and famous journalists; but if it does not address harassment by restaurant owners, construction foremen, and college administrators, it will fail. Thus far, the situation does not look promising.

Sexual Harassment Will Be Sharply Reduced in the Future

"I'm sure the road will be long and difficult, but it will be positive in the end."

—French journalist Sandra Muller

Quoted in Stephanie Zacharek, Eliana Dockterman, and Haley Sweetland Edwards, "Person of the Year 2017. The Silence Breakers," *Time*, December 18, 2017. http://time.com.

Consider these questions as you read:

1. What does the mention of Time's Up add to this essay? How would the argument be weaker if Time's Up was not included?
2. The author notes that *Time*'s Person of the Year award for 2017 was given to "the Silence Breakers." How does this fact support the argument?
3. After reading both this essay and the previous one, do you think sexual harassment will be reduced in the future? Why or why not? Cite a piece of evidence that swayed you.

Editor's note: The discussion that follows presents common arguments made in support of this perspective, reinforced by facts, quotes, and examples taken from various sources.

For many years, public accusations against bosses who sexually harassed their employees were rare; when these accusations did surface, they were largely ignored. Few perpetrators ever lost their jobs for harassing their employees; few even had their reputations damaged. In 2017 and 2018, however, people who alleged they had been harassed by rich and powerful men such as Kevin Spacey, Matt Lauer, and Harvey Weinstein received a very different response. They were *believed*. Moreover, their example led other victims to speak out about the harassment they received, and their accusations ultimately formed a coherent movement dedicated to eliminating sexual harassment. These events represent a watershed moment in the way Americans view harassment. They have forever changed the world.

Warnings and Punishments

There are several reasons to believe that sexual harassment will become increasingly rare. Perhaps the best reason involves what has happened to men like Spacey and Lauer. They have been humiliated, fired from their jobs, and some have even lost their fortunes; their names are now worthless. The fates of these men stand as a warning to other powerful and wealthy people who might be tempted to sexually harass others. As an editorial in the *Chicago Tribune* puts it, "When a guy named Harvey Weinstein is suddenly fired from a company called the Weinstein Company, it should serve as a blaring alert to every powerful person in America who has preyed on less powerful people: Don't think you can avoid the consequences."[55]

Sexual harassers have long relied on intimidation to keep their victims from speaking out. In the era of #MeToo, however, harassers can no longer expect their victims to stay silent. Today Americans are increasingly likely to speak up when they have been harassed, and they are far more likely than ever to be believed when they do. Every potential harasser must surely be aware that harassment is no longer an easy secret to keep. Especially in the entertainment industry, the odds are excellent that such treatment will eventually come to light. That knowledge is a strong incentive for even the richest, most powerful men to avoid situations in which they might be exposed as harassers.

This does not imply that sexual harassment is a thing of the past.

> "When a guy named Harvey Weinstein is suddenly fired from a company called the Weinstein Company, it should serve as a blaring alert to every powerful person in America who has preyed on less powerful people: Don't think you can avoid the consequences."[55]
>
> —A *Chicago Tribune* editorial

Plenty of people behave foolishly, after all, failing to learn from their own mistakes, let alone the mistakes of others. In addition, many people, especially powerful ones, believe they are invulnerable. It is easy for harassers to convince themselves that a victim will never speak up, or that her story will not be believed if she does. But most people, even harassers, are largely rational and will not deliberately put themselves in harm's way. They will pay attention to what happened to harassers and take steps not to suffer the same fate. As a result, the incidence of harassment is likely to begin dropping sharply.

The Success of #MeToo

Other evidence that America has reached a turning point regarding sexual harassment has to do with the meteoric rise of the #MeToo movement. When actress Alyssa Milano asked people to tweet *#MeToo* if they had every been sexually harassed, the response was overwhelming. In the first hour after Milano's request, two hundred thousand people had tweeted *#MeToo*, and 4.7 million used the hashtag on Facebook in the first twenty-four hours. The celebrities who responded included well-known women like Olympic gymnast McKayla Maroney, actresses Gwyneth Paltrow and Viola Davis, and singer Lady Gaga. The movement quickly spread from its American origins to other nations, and the phrase *#MeToo* has been translated into dozens of languages.

The #MeToo movement, moreover, has already had an enormous impact on society. Each December, *Time* magazine selects a Person of the Year, a designation that acknowledges the individual or group that has "done the most to influence the events of the year."[56] Past winners have included activists such as Martin Luther King Jr. and Mahatma Gandhi, business leaders such as Facebook cofounder Mark

> "The world is listening."[57]
>
> —A *Time* magazine article on activists against sexual harassment

Zuckerberg, and groups such as peacemakers and philanthropists. In 2017 *Time* chose "the Silence Breakers" as Person of the Year, highlighting the women who founded #MeToo along with others who are demanding

Awareness and Condemnation of Sexual Harassment Are Increasing

In 2011 an ABC News/*Washington Post* survey revealed that 64 percent of Americans viewed sexual harassment in the workplace as a problem, with 47 percent calling it a serious problem. A similar survey done in 2017 demonstrated an increase in both these figures: 75 percent called harassment a problem, and 64 percent called it a serious problem. The trend is evident: people are increasingly willing to see sexual harassment as a problem.

Sexual Harassment Survey Answers, 2011 and 2017

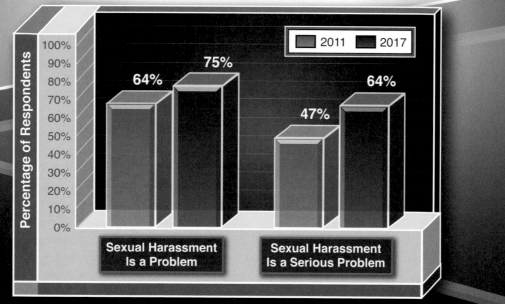

Source: Claire Zillman, "A New Poll on Sexual Harassment Suggests Why 'Me Too' Went So Insanely Viral," *Fortune,* October 17, 2017. http://fortune.com.

an end to sexual harassment. "The world is listening,"[57] *Time*'s cover story concluded.

The #MeToo movement was at first sometimes described as a blip or a fad, but it is neither. As a grassroots organization that makes excellent use of social media to keep itself in the public eye, #MeToo has struck a chord among millions of Americans, both men and women. In many ways it resembles other successful social movements, perhaps most notably the women's rights movement of the 1960s and 1970s. Like #MeToo, that movement galvanized women across the country who were concerned about sexism and wanted new economic and social opportunities. Though women still face many issues today, there is no question that the feminist movement brought women's issues into the mainstream and changed the way both women and men thought about the role of women in society. #MeToo appears to be following a similar path.

Leaders and Goals

Some argue that #MeToo is fatally flawed because it is a decentralized movement with no clear leaders and unfocused goals. But it is simply untrue that all successful social movements have easily identifiable leaders. One example is the gay rights movement, which has been one of the most successful social movements in history. For many years LGBT people were marginalized, despised, and feared, with many going to great lengths to hide their sexual orientation from families and employers. As recently as 1974 the psychiatric community viewed homosexuality as a form of mental illness. For years after that, people were fired, beaten, or ostracized for being gay, and those who chose to live with romantic partners could not enjoy the legal benefits of marriage.

By 2018, though, the landscape had changed dramatically. Although prejudice against LGBT people certainly remains, tolerance and acceptance of gay rights is higher than ever. Same-sex couples have the right to marry in every state, corporations target advertising toward the gay and lesbian market, and increasingly fewer people feel a need to hide their sexuality. Yet the gay rights movement achieved these goals despite having few, if any, recognizable leaders, and certainly no one who has achieved fame on the level of Martin Luther King Jr. or Susan B. Anthony. Clearly, then, #MeToo can be successful without centralized leadership.

Nor is it accurate to argue that #MeToo lacks coherent goals. On the contrary, the movement has a very specific set of objectives: to call attention to the issue of sexual harassment and assault, especially by reassuring victims that they are not alone and that they can survive and heal. As Milano put it, tweeting *#MeToo* would "give people a sense of the magnitude of the problem."[58] In this way, the movement continues to be a huge success. By focusing on the issue of sexual assault and harassment, #MeToo succeeds in engaging and energizing millions of women—a process that can lead to changes in the hearts and minds of the American public.

> "[Time's Up] can be thought of as a solution-based, action-oriented next step in the #Metoo movement."[59]
>
> — Journalist Alix Langone

Finally, although #MeToo is not primarily focused on legal issues, those working against sexual harassment do have specific goals for changing the law. This is especially true of an organization called Time's Up, which, according to journalist Alix Langone, "can be thought of as a solution-based, action-oriented next step in the #Metoo movement."[59] Time's Up works toward legislation that would make workplaces more equitable—such as equal pay for equal work—and would thus reduce the amount of power men have over women in a typical working environment. These goals are achievable with work and persistence.

It is simply not the case, then, that the antiharassment movement has no clear purpose. Quite the opposite: its goals are realistic, clear, and easy to understand, and they make the #MeToo movement more likely to succeed.

Source Notes

Overview: Sexual Harassment in the Spotlight

1. Quoted in Jodi Kantor and Megan Twohey, "Harvey Weinstein Paid Off Sexual Harassment Accusers for Decades," *New York Times*, October 5, 2017. www.nytimes.com.
2. Quoted in BBC News, "Harvey Weinstein Timeline: How the Scandal Unfolded," February 12, 2018. www.bbc.com.
3. Quoted in Kantor and Twohey, "Harvey Weinstein Paid Off Sexual Harassment Accusers for Decades."
4. Todd S. Purdum, "Axis of Harassment: Hollywood, Washington, and the Media Confront Their Demons," Politico, November 30, 2017. www.politico.com.
5. Quoted in Julia Carpenter, "Sexual Harassment Tipping Point: Why Now?," CNN, November 21, 2017. http://money.cnn.com.
6. Equal Employment Opportunity Commission, "Facts About Sexual Harassment." www.eeoc.gov.
7. Quoted in *USA Today*, "Kevin Spacey Apologizes After Actor Accuses Him of Sexual Harassment, Comes Out as Gay," October 30, 2017. www.usatoday.com.
8. Quoted in Anabel Munoz, "Former Staffer Details Groping Incident by Bell Gardens Assemblywoman Cristina Garcia," ABC7 Eyewitness News, February 9, 2018. http://abc7.com.
9. Quoted in Kantor and Twohey, "Harvey Weinstein Paid Off Sexual Harassment Accusers for Decades."

Chapter One: Who Is to Blame for Sexual Harassment?

10. Quoted in Linda Massarella and Laura Italiano, "Hollywood's Horror Stories of Sex Predators Long Before Weinstein," *New York Post*, October 16, 2017. https://nypost.com.
11. Elizabeth Cobbs, "Why the Pulitzer Prize Committee Keeps Ignoring Women's History," *Washington Post*, April 13, 2018. www.washingtonpost.com.
12. Farva Jafri, "Women Don't Speak Up, Because Nobody Listens," *Medium*, April 16, 2018. https://medium.com.
13. Jafri, "Women Don't Speak Up, Because Nobody Listens."
14. Quoted in Daniel Greenfield, "'That's Just Charlie Being Charlie': Sexual

Harassment Scandal Claims Charlie Rose," *FrontPage*, November 21, 2017. www.frontpagemag.com.

15. Kantor and Twohey, "Harvey Weinstein Paid Off Sexual Harassment Accusers for Decades."

16. Quoted in *Nation*, "6 Perspectives on the Future of #MeToo," January 1–8, 2018. www.thenation.com.

17. Richard G. Bribiescas, "Evolution Expert: 'Boys Will Be Boys' Doesn't Explain Sexual Harassment," *Time*, December 7, 2017. http://time.com.

18. Quoted in Ellen Hendriksen, "Four Psychological Traits of Sexual Harassers," *How to Be Yourself* (blog), *Psychology Today*, November 9, 2017. www.psychologytoday.com.

19. Sally Kohn, "Weinstein's Fall Grew from Rage over Trump," CNN, October 20, 2017. www.cnn.com.

20. Quoted in Stephanie Pappas, "Him Too: Who Are the Sexual Harassers?," LiveScience, October 27, 2017. www.livescience.com.

21. Hendriksen, "Four Psychological Traits of Sexual Harassers."

Chapter Two: How Harshly Should Harassers Be Punished?

22. Quoted in Andrea Mandell and Bryan Alexander, "The Oscar Odds for Harvey Weinstein's Award Movies Now Look Dim," *USA Today*, October 11, 2017. www.usatoday.com.

23. Quoted in Josh Rottenberg and Yvonne Villarreal, "Kevin Spacey's Unprecedented Fall from Grace Tests a Stunned Hollywood," *Los Angeles Times*, November 9, 2017. www.latimes.com.

24. Quoted in Michelle Cottle, "Leon Wieseltier: A Reckoning," *Atlantic*, October 27, 2017. www.theatlantic.com.

25. Quoted in Rod Dreher, "Wieseltier and G.H.W. Bush Get Harveyed," *American Conservative*, October 25, 2017. www.theamericanconservative.com.

26. Quoted in David Sims, "'It Was Clearly Intended to Be Funny but Wasn't,'" *Atlantic*, November 16, 2017. www.theatlantic.com.

27. Quoted in Jennifer Brooks and Maya Rao, "Majority of Minnesotans Believe Franken Accusations, but Fewer Think He Should Have Quit," *Minneapolis Star-Tribune*, January 16, 2018. www.startribune.com.

28. Dreher, "Wieseltier and G.H.W. Bush Get Harveyed."

29. Quoted in Cathy Young, "Is 'Weinsteining' Getting Out of Hand?," *Los Angeles Times*, November 1, 2017. www.latimes.com.

30. Quoted in Caroline Framke, "Shaun White Was Sued for Sexual Harassment. NBC Would Rather Not Talk About It," Vox, February 14, 2018. www.vox.com.

31. Quoted in Framke, "Shaun White Was Sued for Sexual Harassment."
32. Dylan Hernandez, "Shaun White Is Surviving His #MeToo Moment," *Los Angeles Times*, February 17, 2018. www.latimes.com.
33. David A. Farenthold, "Trump Recorded Having Extremely Lewd Conversation About Women in 2005," *Washington Post*, October 7, 2016. www.washingtonpost.com.
34. Jeff A. Green, "A Growing Number of Sexual Harassment Cases Are Fading," Bloomberg, April 23, 2018. www.bloomberg.com.
35. Quoted in Stuart Miller, "Louis C.K.'s Path to a Comeback Likely Runs Through Comedy Clubs," *Hollywood Reporter*, April 17, 2018. www.hollywoodreporter.com.
36. Maggie Schmitt, "Sexual Harassment of ANY Kind Is Serious," *Odyssey*, January 3, 2018. www.theodysseyonline.com.
37. Quoted in ABC News, "Matt Damon Says No-One Is Talking About Men Who Are Not Sexual Predators," December 18, 2017. www.abc.net.au.

Chapter Three: Are We Too Quick to Assume That Accused Harassers Are Guilty?

38. Quoted in Yohana Desta, "Morgan Spurlock Reveals History of Sexual Misconduct," *Vanity Fair*, December 14, 2017. www.vanityfair.com.
39. Quoted in Dan Corey, "Since Weinstein, Here's a Growing List of Men Accused of Sexual Misconduct," NBC News, November 8, 2017. www.nbcnews.com.
40. Legal Information Institute, "Presumption of Innocence," Cornell Law School. www.law.cornell.edu.
41. Quoted in Corey, "Since Weinstein, Here's a Growing List of Men Accused of Sexual Misconduct."
42. Quoted in Hunter Harris, "Tom Brokaw Likens Sexual Harassment Accusation to 'Drive-By Shooting' in Leaked Email," Cut, April 27, 2018. www.thecut.com.
43. Quoted in Amanda Arnold, "65 Women in Media Sign Letter in Support of Tom Brokaw," Cut, April 29, 2018. www.thecut.com.
44. Quoted in Stephanie Zacharek, Eliana Dockterman, and Haley Sweetland Edwards, "Person of the Year 2017: The Silence Breakers," *Time*, December 18, 2017. http://time.com.
45. Quoted in Alex Ritman, "Angela Lansbury Says Women 'Must Sometimes Take Blame' for Sexual Harassment," *Hollywood Reporter*, November 28, 2017. www.hollywoodreporter.com.
46. Quoted in Georgea Kovanis, "How Can Sexual Harassment End If Women Keep Blaming the Victim?," *Detroit Free Press*, October 16, 2017. www.freep.com.

47. Quoted in Glenn Whipp, "38 Women Have Come Forward to Accuse Director James Toback of Sexual Harassment," *Los Angeles Times*, October 22, 2017. www.latimes.com.

Chapter Four: Will Sexual Harassment Remain a Significant Problem in the Future?

48. Quoted in Ben Moreell, "Power Corrupts," *Religion and Liberty*, July 20, 2010. https://acton.org.
49. Mary Slaughter, Khalil Smith, and David Rock, "The Brain Science That Could Help Explain Sexual Harassment," *Quartz*, January 24, 2018. https://work.qz.com.
50. Quoted in Slaughter, Smith, and Rock, "The Brain Science That Could Help Explain Sexual Harassment."
51. Quoted in Zacharek, Dockterman, and Edwards, "Person of the Year 2017."
52. Andy Ostroy, "The Failure of Occupy Wall Street," *Huffington Post*, December 6, 2017. www.huffingtonpost.com.
53. Jack Tuckner, "#MeToo Not Just for Celebrities," Tucker, Sipser, Weinstock & Sipser, February 16, 2018. https://womensrightsny.com.
54. David Fagin, "Is the #MeToo Movement Just for Outing Celebs and Politicians, or Are Everyday Bosses Next?," *Huffington Post*, December 11, 2017. www.huffingtonpost.com.
55. *Chicago Tribune*, "Weinstein Case Is a Warning to Sexual Predators: Change or Leave," October 9, 2017. www.chicagotribune.com.
56. Quoted in Caroline McCarthy, "Mark Zuckerberg Named Time's Person of the Year," CNET, December 15, 2010. www.cnet.com.
57. Zacharek, Dockterman, and Edwards, "Person of the Year 2017."
58. Quoted in Sophie Gilbert, "The Movement of #MeToo," *Atlantic*, October 16, 2017. www.theatlantic.com.
59. Alix Langone, "#MeToo and Time's Up Founders Explain the Difference Between the 2 Movements—and How They're Alike," *Time*, March 8, 2018. http://time.com.

Sexual Harassment Facts

History of Sexual Harassment

- The term *sexual harassment* was popularized in 1974 by Lin Farley, a journalist who taught that year at Cornell University in New York.
- The 1976 legal case *Williams v. Saxbe* established that firing employees for turning down a supervisor's sexual or romantic overtures was sex discrimination and therefore illegal.
- In 1991 Supreme Court nominee Clarence Thomas was accused of sexual harassment by his former employee Anita Hill, bringing the term *sexual harassment* into the mainstream.
- The phrase *Me Too* was coined in 2006 by Tarana Burke, who worked with young sexual assault victims in Alabama.
- The hashtag *#MeToo* became famous as a result of a tweet by actress Alyssa Milano in October 2017.

Definitions of Sexual Harassment

- Both men and women can be perpetrators of sexual harassment, and both can be targets of harassment as well.
- A sexual harasser is often a supervisor of the victim, but he or she may also be a coworker or even a nonemployee (delivery person, custodian, etc.).
- Sexual harassment may include comments directed at victims because of their gender, even if they are not sexual in nature.
- Most types of sexual harassment are not considered crimes, but victims may sue for damages in civil court.

US Statistics

- According to US Equal Employment Opportunity Commission (EEOC) statistics, as of 2017 about 15 percent of all victims of sexual harassment in the workplace ever file a formal complaint with the police or other authority figure.

- A 2018 poll by an organization called Stop Street Harassment reveals that 81 percent of American women have experienced sexual harassment at some point in their lives.
- EEOC data from 2017 reveals that a high percentage of American women have experienced sexual harassment at work.
- According to EEOC data from 2017, about 75 percent of employees who speak out against harassment experience some forms of retaliation afterward.
- A 2017 poll from Quinnipiac University showed that 88 percent of Americans think that sexual harassment is a serious problem.
- Women are at least twice as likely as men to be victims of sexual harassment in the United States, based on data presented by the EEOC.
- About 30 percent of female harassment victims report that the experience made them feel anxious or depressed, according to a 2017 Quinnipiac University poll.

International Statistics

- According to the 2017 Crime Survey of England and Wales, about 20 percent of women in the United Kingdom say they have experienced sexual harassment at work.
- In Vietnam, 87 percent of women polled in 2017 by three nonprofit groups say they have experienced sexual harassment in or out of work.
- In Australia, according to a 2015 poll by the Australia Institute, close to 90 percent of women say they have been verbally harassed in public places, such as while walking on the sidewalk.
- More than 95 percent of women in Cairo, Egypt, say they have been sexually harassed, according to a 2014 poll by a group called Harassmap.

Related Organizations and Websites

A Call to Men
250 Merrick Rd., #813
Rockville Center, NY 11570
website: www.acalltomen.org

A Call to Men works with men to reduce the incidence of sexual misconduct, including harassment. The organization provides educational and training materials to raise awareness of the issue and to encourage men to respect and value women.

American Civil Liberties Union (ACLU)
125 Broad St. Eighteenth Floor
New York, NY 10004
website: www.aclu.org

The ACLU advocates for civil liberties and defends them when they are under attack. Although sexual harassment is not necessarily included under civil rights laws, some of the ACLU's articles and educational materials deal with sexual harassment and other forms of sexual misbehavior.

Equal Opportunity Employment Commission (EEOC)
131 M St., NE
Washington, DC 20507
website: www.eeoc.gov

The EEOC is a federal agency that handles complaints about issues involving the workplace. These include questions regarding sexual harassment. The EEOC's website offers information about sexual harassment on the job.

Girls for Gender Equity
25 Chapel St., Suite 1006
Brooklyn, NY 11201
website: www.ggenyc.org

This organization supports the economic, physical, and psychological development of girls and women, particularly those of color. It is active in the fight against violence, including sexual violence and sexual harassment.

Lean In
855 El Camino Real
Building 5, Suite 307
Palo Alto, CA 94301
website: http://leanin.org

Lean In is an advocacy organization for women. In addition to lobbying for equal pay and working to provide mentors for women and girls, Lean In offers educational materials about sexual harassment and support for those who have experienced it.

me too. movement
website: https://metoomvmt.org

This organization focuses on sexual harassment and other kinds of sexual violence with an emphasis on survivors and healing. Its website includes information about harassment and the organization's work; it also includes many links to other useful sites.

RAINN (Rape, Abuse & Incest National Network)
website: www.rainn.org

RAINN is the largest organization in the United States fighting against sexual assault, including sexual harassment. It provides educational materials and offers support to survivors of sexual abuse and misconduct.

Time's Up

website: www.timesupnow.com

Time's Up focuses on legal remedies for sexual harassment and other sexual misconduct. Originally founded by women in entertainment, it advocates for new laws and enforcement of older laws and policies to ensure the safety of women in the workplace.

For Further Research

Periodicals

David A. Farenthold, "Trump Recorded Having Extremely Lewd Conversation About Women in 2005," *Washington Post*, October 7, 2016. www.washingtonpost.com/politics/trump-recorded-having-extremely-lewd-conversation-about-women-in-2005/2016/10/07/3b9ce776-8cb4-11e6-bf8a-3d26847eeed4_story.html?noredirect=on&utm_term=.cfae7681c855.

Sophie Gilbert, "The Movement of #MeToo," *Atlantic*, October 16, 2017. www.theatlantic.com/entertainment/archive/2017/10/the-movement-of-metoo/542979/.SEFEFS.

Ellen Hendriksen, "Four Psychological Traits of Sexual Harassers," *How to Be Yourself* (blog), *Psychology Today*, November 9, 2017. www.psychologytoday.com/us/blog/how-be-yourself/201711/four-psychological-traits-sexual-harassers.

Jodi Kantor and Megan Twohey, "Harvey Weinstein Paid Off Sexual Harassment Accusers for Decades," *New York Times*, October 5, 2017. www.nytimes.com/2017/10/05/us/harvey-weinstein-harassment-allegations.html.

Nation, "6 Perspectives on the Future of #MeToo," January 1–8, 2018. www.thenation.com/article/6-perspectives-on-the-future-of-metoo.

Cathy Young, "Is 'Weinsteining' Getting Out of Hand?," *Los Angeles Times*, November 1, 2017. www.latimes.com/opinion/op-ed/la-oe-young-weinsteining-goes-too-far-20171101-story.html.

Stephanie Zacharek, Eliana Dockterman, and Haley Sweetland Edwards, "Person of the Year 2017: The Silence Breakers," *Time*, December 18, 2017. http://time.com/time-person-of-the-year-2017-silence-breakers.

Internet Sources

Equal Employment Opportunity Commission, "Facts About Sexual Harassment." www.eeoc.gov/eeoc/publications/fs-sex.cfm.

Farva Jafri, "Women Don't Speak Up, Because Nobody Listens," *Medium*, April 16, 2018. https://medium.com/@farvastra/women-dont-speak-up-because-nobody-listens-83df9746ce2e.

RAINN, "Sexual Harassment." www.rainn.org/articles/sexual-harassment.

Index

Picture Credits

About the Author

Stephen Currie has written many books for young adults and children. His works for ReferencePoint Press include *Sharing Posts: The Spread of Fake News*; *Thinking Critically: Cyberbullying*; *Forgotten Youth: Undocumented Immigrant Youth*; *Teen Guide to Finance: Teen Guide to Saving and Investing*; *Cause & Effect: The Ancient Maya*; and *Issues in the Digital Age: Online Privacy*. He has also taught grade levels ranging from kindergarten to college. He lives in New York's Hudson Valley.